Shooting Stars

&

Origami Swans

Jessica Jaymes Purdy

Reader Cautions

This collection is the story of my life in relation to my identity as a transwoman. It is raw, emotional, and, like life, full of challenging themes and emotions.

Dysphoria haunts these pages as it has haunted my experiences. You will feel my pain, sadness, despair, confusion, and hopelessness. Take heart, though, dear reader; my story has a happy ending. I cannot caution you against any of the poems in this collection based on dysphoria. It is too much a part of my life to think it isn't reflected in every line.

There are some specific cautions I do wish to make because the nature of these poems makes the theme(s) abundantly clear and may be overwhelming or triggering for some.

* Use/mention of homophobic and transphobic slurs.

** Mention or description of self-harm

*** Mention or description of suicide

+ Mention or description of religious trauma and/or persecution

x Sexual or anatomical content

These symbols appear in the titles of poems.

Acknowledgments

I want to offer my deep thanks and love to my family and friends who have loved, supported, and affirmed me through thick and thin. Without them, life would be so much less.

And I also want to thank all the allies and family members who have been there, loving, supporting, and advocating for all my trans and nonbinary siblings. Each of you is a light in a world of shadows.

About the Author

Jessica Jaymes Purdy is a transwoman, poet, activist, and human resources consultant whose journey of self-discovery and transformation has included a series of reinventions of self.

From Son & Brother

To Soldier

To Husband

To Career Ladder Climber

To Full-Time Childcare Giver

To Daughter & Sister

To Diversity, Equity, and Inclusion Consultant

To Activist

Through it all, she has written poetry. She has explored her darkness in her first collection, "Dive Bars & Empty Glasses". And her light. She has explored the beauty and magic of everyday moments in her second collection, "Captured Moments". In her third collection, she explored the social and political realities that so many are suffering under. With her fourth collection, "Glass Hearts & Broken Pedestals," she explored love and romance from her perspective as an asexual, panromantic transwoman. Now, in this collection, "Shooting Stars and Origami Swans" she shares a deeply intimate look into her soul.

Raised in Lancaster, Pennsylvania, she left home to discover herself. Little did she realize how much of herself she would have to discover or how long it would take to embrace her authentic self. 25 years after leaving, Jessica would return to Lancaster a new woman, rediscovering the hometown she'd sworn she'd never move back to. Though it had changed for the better, she had changed more.

She's found herself, her place, and her people. Her poetry is a gift she offers to the world in the hope that it will help others find themselves, their place, and their people just as the words she spilled across so many pages as she's worked through her thoughts, beliefs, struggles, and emotions have helped her find hers.

Foreword

It has taken me years to find the words for Shooting Stars and Origami Swans. And once I finally found them, I found myself struggling to find a way to introduce this collection. I'm overwhelmed by the flood of emotions as I contemplate these poems, nearly overwhelmed by fear and anxiety because this isn't just another poetry collection — it's my soul laid bare.

Poetry has always been my refuge, my confessional, my battle cry. It's how I've made sense of my emotions and the world. But this collection? It's different. It's raw. It's real. It's my life. The parts of me that I've always protected most fiercely.

When I started editing this collection, I was drowning in words. Hundreds of pages of poems, prose, and late-night scribbles stared back at me, each piece a fragment of my truth. Choosing which to include was like picking through the shards of a broken mirror — each an important part of my life, my journey, but not all able to fit into the gilded frame.

I'm going to be real with you here, just as I am in the poems you will soon experience — this isn't an easy read. There are poems here that still make my heart ache, that drown me in the emotions of the moments they captured. You'll find anger here, and frustration. You'll find the kind of sadness that sits heavy in your bones and the pain that comes from being unseen, unheard, misunderstood. You'll meet the ghost of my dysphoria, which haunts these pages as it's haunted my life.

But that's not the whole story. Not by a long shot.

Because woven through these pages, like golden threads in a tapestry, you'll also find joy. Hope. Love. The kind of strength that comes from being knocked down a thousand times and getting up a thousand and one. You'll find beauty in the most unexpected places — in the cracks, in the scars, in the pieces that don't quite fit but are perfect in their imperfection.

Some of these poems might feel unfinished to you or repetitive; this collection might seem a little all over the place. That's intentional. Because life — real, messy, beautiful life — doesn't follow a neat, linear path. It loops back on itself; it takes detours. It surprises you. My journey has been a meandering wander, constantly moving but often looping back to lessons I thought I'd already learned, seeing them with new eyes each time.

I've organized this collection into chapters, each one a snapshot of a different part of my journey. "Unloved" delves into the dark places, the experiences of rejection and exclusion that so many of us face. "The Hidden Self" explores what it means to live behind a mask, to hide your truth from the world and sometimes even from yourself.

But we don't stay in the shadows forever. "Dreams of Freedom" is about that first spark of hope, that moment when you dare to imagine a different life. "A Warrior Born" chronicles the battle to become who you truly are, while "Defiance" is a rallying cry, a refusal to be silenced or pushed aside.

And finally, "A Joyful Woman" — because, yes, there is joy. There is triumph. There is a life beyond the struggle, even if the echoes of that struggle never fully fade away.

This collection is my soul laid bare. It's the ocean of tears I've shed, the brightest smiles I've smiled, and the mountains of doubt I've conquered. It's my offering to you — whether you're on a similar journey or whether you're trying to understand someone who is.

These are my shooting stars, my origami swans. My wishes made manifest, my hopes folded into delicate shapes and set free on the wind. May they find their way to those who need them most.

You are at the threshold of my soul. Welcome.

Unloved

Jessica Jaymes Purdy

Things That Don't Kill You

I was bullied when I was young,

couldn't make my gender fit.

I was illiterate in the ways of

open vulnerability and deep truths.

I was drowning in depression;

scaled mountains in fear.

I didn't know who I was

when I flung myself from the nest,

a fragile egg, yet to find my wings.

I shattered upon the hard reality of hate,

drank poison like it was medicine,

ate pills like Alice trying to escape Wonderland.

I fought my way into the closet -

through the wardrobe of manhood,

past icy landscapes and lampposts of hope

that quickly disappeared into a forest

dense with denial and dissociation -

fantasizing that I was still living my life.

Shooting Stars & Origami Swans

I married for the love of expectation,

balanced my powerlessness against a toxic strength

that I had learned to survive in others

until I had adapted to its harsh environment

and become a creature of silent pain;

finding solace in fractured realities.

I sculpted a mosaic of the life I believed was my destiny

in the heavy stone of societal norms,

tethered my life raft-self to hangover cliffs

after high-pressure days that raged

 like storms through the darkness within

until I was stripped bare like a winter tree waiting for the fire.

I shattered into nothingness

beneath the sledgehammer blows

of a love that needed my weakness

until I could no longer offer a spine

upon which to center the target.

I lost the image of me in that pulverizing love.

Jessica Jaymes Purdy

I haunted the ruins of my life like a ghost;

drank liquid fire, thinking I could reignite something inside,

torching everything in my path instead.

I dove off the cliffs, drowned in despair,

washed up on the shores of a life I did not desire.

I was a castaway, lost in the vast ocean of hopelessness.

I was an empty shell devoid of the life that once called it home.

People could still hear whispers of me

like the sound of a long-dead sea -

all desolation and salted wounds.

Like driftwood, the tides of life carried me

on waves to shores of pain and healing.

I shrunk in on myself until I became a dense, ripe seed

taking root in the dark soil of time-heals-all-wounds;

a lie that placates with a kernel of truth.

I healed in time, not through time.

I healed just enough wounds

to blossom into myself.

Holy Until[+]

5

I am holy.

My body sacred.

My love, a prayer.

I am a child of the divine.

I am a miracle made manifest.

I am holy.

Until your love washes over me.

Until your prayers drown me beneath your faith.

Until your church lays its foundation over my life.

Until your graveyard of grace buries me in sins that are not mine.

Jessica Jaymes Purdy

Princess

They called me princess.

They meant it as an insult.

Little did they know it was a powerful dream.

It's Not About That[+]

It's not about you being a Republican.

It's about you believing I don't deserve equal rights.

It's not about you being a Christian.

It's about you using it to justify bigotry.

It's not about a difference of opinion.

It's about you believing I have no right to be who I am.

Jessica Jaymes Purdy

National Coming Out Day

I'm already out.

I announced my transition

I told you about my rising feminine

That I was folding my masculinity

And putting it away forever.

But every day, I have to come out again.

    And again.

How can I not when who I was is not who I am

And the hiring manager asks who is he?

When a caller says hello, sir?

When the server sees stubble over dinner?

How can I not when the doctor needs to know

So they can remind me to turn my head and cough?

Or screen me for cancers men might get?

When the insurance says women can't need an Orchiectomy?

Shooting Stars & Origami Swans

How can I not when the pharmacist fills my Estrogen?

Or the TSA agent is staring at a flag

And pulling me aside for a pat down?

When they all do a double take when I speak?

It's National Coming Out Day.

Just like every other day.

Jessica Jaymes Purdy

I Shouldn't Have

I shouldn't have listened to the people who told me

I was a sick freak unworthy of life or love

I shouldn't have made their voices my own.

I shouldn't have chained myself in a cell of my own making.

I shouldn't have tortured and abused myself

Until I made myself into a reflection of their words.

I shouldn't have survived but I did, many times over.

I shouldn't have waited so long to say,

"Fuck the shouldn'ts,"

And finally, allow myself happiness and self-love.

Where Not Caring Means I Cannot Go

Sometimes I pass

Mostly, when I stay silent

Almost always before two

And it matters

Sometimes I don't pass

Like when I speak

Or when my stubble grows

And I don't care

I've chosen to be visible

So, most of the time, I don't worry

But I'm careful about where

My not caring means I cannot go

Jessica Jaymes Purdy

Why do you?

Why do you fear me?

The ways in which we differ;

The way I honor the deep truths

Of my soul in defiance of expectations?

Why do you hate me?

For knowing myself better

Than our binary society ever could;

For choosing to live rather than giving in?

Why do you not see me?

As a person worthy of respect;

Someone deserving of the same rights

As a cisgendered person, as someone like you?

Imminent Failure Warning

The alarm is going off,
But all I hear is screaming
And I struggle to thrust myself
Upward and break from the orbit
Of sleep and dreams of days I do not
Hate the way I've come to hate work week
Days that force me into an office where I will
Once more be faced with a boss who despises me
For daring to exist, for daring to live, for transitioning
From the man he disliked into to the woman he denies
That I truly am, who wants nothing more than to push me
Out of his sight, out of his thoughts, out of his office completely.

The weight of having to deal with this reality
Is an inescapable gravity well surrounding
A black hole of fear, and worry, and stress
That builds like the red red-hot pressure
Of a rocket engine exceeding
Its designed safety limits
As it struggles to rise
Above the event
Horizon before
It completely
Destroys
Itself.

You Don't Have To Understand

Transitioning is about more than bringing my body into alignment

With my soul. It's about more than anatomy.

It's about authenticity.

It's about embracing myself.

It's about living rather than existing.

It's about truly being happy in a way that I could never be before.

You don't need to understand what makes me transgender.

You don't have to understand how I know that I'm transgender.

You don't have to understand what being transgender feels like.

You don't have to understand why I waited to transition.

You don't need to understand everything, or even anything

Involved in transitioning.

The only thing you need to understand

Is embracing my authentic self brings me peace and joy.

Dear God[+]

I know that I'm not a mistake,

That love resides all around

If only I could open my eyes and see.

But I'm afraid of what I might find.

It seems that hate has found fertile ground

And grown thickets of barbed vines

That will strangle and bleed me to death.

So many say that I should not exist,

That I am an affront to your splendor and glory,

That I am a broken mistake to be beaten

Into their narrow view of your Garden of Eden.

And yes, God, I know that I'm not a follower

Of any of your churches, but still,

I'm asking you to break your long silence

And speak with a voice that even the deafest might hear.

I'm asking you to say that love was always the way.

That love is still the way and always shall be.

I'm asking you to preach tolerance and respect in person once more,

Because your voice has so often been twisted

By the pride of those who preach in your name.

Please, God, tell the world I'm not a mistake.

Unforgivable

I thought I was unknowable

Because I never allowed myself to be seen

I hid in the shadows

Blended into the light

I lived in half breaths

Fearing your sight

For I ever was what all your words

Said was unforgivable

Jessica Jaymes Purdy

You Speak of Love[+]

You speak of love

As if it is the sweet nectar of

God made manifest

But the love you offer

It's like fruit rotten on the vine

Its roots dark, twisted, lifeless

Within your heart

You speak of love

Like a shield against hate

Prayerfully offered to all

But it's a heavy spiked weapon

Of a war waged in God's name

That batters, bruises, breaks the souls

Of the defenseless.

Shooting Stars & Origami Swans

You speak of love

As if you do not wield it

Like a weapon

A sword cutting deep

Into the souls of those

You believe need to be saved

Before casting them out

Jessica Jaymes Purdy

The Choice

Sitting in a room full of chatter

Aromatic coffee adding ambiance

To the trendy music weaving

Through conversations

And I'm waiting

For no one

Because they are all here

And our laughter is ringing

Joyously, through the air

But I'm waiting

As the insistence grows

For the need to build

To a crescendo pitch

And I can no longer wait

To make the choice

Between men's or women's

To have need override fear

A substitute for bravery

So I'm waiting

Before, I have to face

The stares of strangers

And the possibility

Of cruel words cutting

Confidence and happiness

To shreds of despair

So I'm waiting

Jessica Jaymes Purdy

Praying For Me[+]

You say you want to pray for me

But you are not praying for my best interest

You are praying for me

To change

You're praying for me

To be something that I am not

You are praying for me

To be something that you will be comfortable with

You are praying for me

To shape myself into something

That causes me discomfort

So that you don't have to

Experience any of your own

You are praying at me

How Do You

How do you know when you are enough?

When every word you hear tells you that you are not

How do you learn your worth?

When every word you hear tells you that you are worthless

How do you hold on to the woman inside?

When every word you hear tells you - you are a man

How do you live your truth?

When every word you hear tells you that it is a lie

How do you learn to love yourself?

When every word you hear tells you that you are hated

How do you go on living?

When every word you hear tells you that you should just die

The Hidden Self

What Is This[x]

This.
What is this?

This thing

That dangles and wobbles;
That grows and moves
Between my legs?

Why does it beg?
For attention?

Not this.
Please.

I never wanted this.

Hey God
Are you there?
Are you awake?

Is your hearing aid in?
Can you hear me?

This
Why this?

This isn't mine.

You've made a mistake
And given me
Someone else's gift.

It doesn't fit.
It's just not for me.

This.
Not this.

Please God never this.

Un-Reflected

There's a version of me reflected in the mirror

A me that is at once recognizable and utterly alien

It's the version that the world thinks it sees

But that I know has never truly been me

I see in the mirror a reflection I've known for life

A reflection not of me but of the part I play

For in that reflection I cannot find my soul

For my soul has never been visible to the eyes of the world

Jessica Jaymes Purdy

It Starts As A Whisper

It starts as a whisper

    A secret

    This tiny truth

Kept hidden in the shadow

Of who you pretend to be

You fight it, wrestle it

    Chain it down

    So it doesn't escape

    Into the light for others to see

It starts as a whisper

    Insistent,

    Urgent

Refusing to be denied

It raises it's voice

Muzzle it, gag it

    Keep it as silent as death

    So no one ever hears

    The truth behind who they see

It's louder now, its screaming
        So hard to believe
        That no one else has ever seen
        The mask of yourself slip away

It's louder now, its screaming

Jessica Jaymes Purdy

Who Am I[x]

Who am I?

Am I the body you see?

The cock and balls

Assumed and unseen?

Am I the man I pretend?

The clothes that he wears?

The job he attends?

Who am I?

Am I the woman that I dream?

The body I wish were mine?

The clothes I wish to wear?

Who am I?

Am I a soul trapped?

A being doomed

To be neither one or the other?

Who am I?
31

Am I the name given at birth?
The name that I would choose?
Am I just a gendered pronoun?

Who am I?

Am I the memory of the past?
The future yet to come?
Am I now who I am?

Who am I?

Jessica Jaymes Purdy

Hidey Home

I live my life behind locked doors
With the curtains drawn
Breathing artificial air
Hidden within my home
From prying judgmental eyes

Crack the door open just enough
To slide out into character
Playing the man
That you all expect me to be
Living a hundred painful lies

Fall through the door exhausted
Leave my costume on the floor
The lonely girl awakes
And dreams of days
That seem to be forever far away

To throw open the windows
             And walk out the door

             Confident and proud

To escape the safety

Of my hidey home

Jessica Jaymes Purdy

I'm Ill-Fitting

I wear myself like a suit

Taken out of dad's closet when I twelve

I'm ill-fitting and slightly absurd

Feel like I'm playing dress-up

That's this is all pretend

I'm a character in my own life

Like I'm a performance

Taking place on an eternal stage

Feels like I'm more of a lie

Than an actor pretending

An Empty Suit

Spend my days looking

For a place to exist

Within my own skin

Where mind and body

And soul all agree

Spend my days feeling

Like an empty suit

A costume on a mannequin

How can I be real?

When my body seems so fake

Jessica Jaymes Purdy

Pretending Manhood

All my time pretending

I'm a character in my own life

Every day a performance

For everyone else's benefit

All my time pretending

My entire life a mask

Worn as a shield

Protection from discovery

All my time pretending

Nothing ever feels real

Every day a stranger in the mirror

What truth remains to believe?

Brave Desire

Brave

I've never desired

To be

The desire

That resides within

My heart

Is simply

To be free to live

As myself

Jessica Jaymes Purdy

Easier

It's easier not to be

Brave

Simpler to stay

Silent

But who does that

Save

How do you live?

Shooting Stars and Origami Swans

It came without warning,

That moment when everything

Was no longer enough

And the truth came crashing

Through the roof, punching

Itself into my life like a Shooting Star

Wish birthing itself in my soul.

How many stars died?

With my wishes tattooed

Upon their shining surfaces?

How many times had I folded

My hope into origami swans

And released them to chase the stars?

So many that I no longer believed.

And so it came without warning,

A moment where the wish must fall

And take its place within my life;

A moment when its failure to appear

Was no longer an option to bear.

And, as the house of my forbearance

Burned to ash, I rose from my own fires.

You'll Be 40, But. . .

To my younger self,

You'll be 40, but. . .

You will find your courage. You will find your voice. You will recognize your strength.

You will feel guilty about not having been brave in your twenties. Don't. You weren't ready. You didn't have the strength then. You would likely have become a sad statistic.

There are a few things that you need to know. First, each of us walks a different path. None of those paths are wrong. Second, any regret you feel, put it aside. You had a good life, and you will become the woman you were meant to be. Third, Mom, Dad and your brother will all be supportive. You can count on them and your closest friends to have your back.

You are beautiful. You are loved. You are strong.

Love,

Jessi

Jessica Jaymes Purdy

Was I Honest?

I called myself honest;

Claimed that I was a truthful person.

But was I?

I hid my secret

Behind closed closet doors.

Wore masks.

I pretended

To be myself for everyone.

But where was I?

I was buried

Deep beneath the expectations

I let you believe.

Shooting Stars & Origami Swans

I lived my life

While allowing you to believe my lie.

Where was my honesty?

Where was it then

When I was not authentic to myself?

I was lying to myself,

Pretending I was

Exactly who I was supposed to be.

How was that honest?

Jessica Jaymes Purdy

Razor Blade

How I hate the sound of blade on hair.

Like

The

Soft

Whisper

Of

The

Nylon

Zipper

Of

My

Army

Sweats

Reminding me

Of all the times

The drill instructor

Barked "Man up ladies"

As I grew more exhausted

Shooting Stars & Origami Swans

From being all that I should be

Like

The

Sound

Of

Velcro

Pulling

Before

Taking

Off

The

Brace

That

Held

Me

In

Place

Forever having

To strip away the

Masculinity of birth

Reminded every morning

That I am both more and less

Than the image seen in the mirror

Like

The

Sound

Of

Sandpaper

In

Geppetto's

Hand

As

He

Lovingly

Crafted

Pinocchio

Never realizing

He'd forever dream

Shooting Stars & Origami Swans

Of being real just like

My dream of forever leaving

Behind the wooden marionette

Of my birth who danced on others' strings

Oh, how I hate the sound of blade on hair.

Jessica Jaymes Purdy

When I Die

When I die

Do not bury the body

The bones will linger

Telling lies about my life

Truths I'd rather not share

Not even after life

When I die

Do not bury the body

Light a sacred fire

Let the ash claim my secrets

Tell the story of my living

Spread my stories on the wind

Where Does One Live? ***

Where does one live

When your own body

Doesn't feel like home

When you've been fenced in

Kept out of the spaces

Your soul longs to visit

Where does one live

When you can't afford the keys

To the body you wish was yours

When your own body

Feels like betrayal

And simply doesn't fit

You live in dreams

Of 'maybes' and 'one days'

In secret moments

Jessica Jaymes Purdy

50

You live in silence

In fear and shame

In closets shut tight

You live in the shadow

Of sorrow and despair

In thoughts of suicide

The Closet Of Masculinity**

My gender identity
Didn't change when I started puberty

It didn't change when I joined the army

It didn't change when I separated under
Don't Ask Don't Tell

It didn't change when I climbed deeper into
The closet of masculinity

It didn't change when I got married.

I didn't shed my gender identity
Like a Halloween costume after the ball

I just learned to hide it

Mostly
Sometimes
Maybe not quite

Jessica Jaymes Purdy

I was never a happy, healthy cis man.

I was a drug user
Bordering on addict

I was a heavy drinker
Many called an alcoholic

I have scars from my depression that didn't quite kill me

I was still living

But I'd been defeated
I'd given up

Death was coming slowly
100 pounds overweight and shuffling
Towards a broken ravaged heart

This Body[x]

This body, my body, male-born body

This body sparked by sperm pierced egg

Growing cell by cell within a female body

A body mine recognized as mother

And also as mirrored reflection of itself

This body, my body, male-born body

This body, small, weak, and wailing body

Maleness protruding, identified boy body

A boy body, only to be dressed in blue body

To grow up into muscular, hairy man body

This body, my body, male-born body

Transgender body lost deep in masculinity

This body, a fun house mirror parody body

A stranger's body seeing ghostly reflections

Drowning in a testosterone hormone stew

Jessica Jaymes Purdy

This body, my body, male-born body

This body, ill-fitting, ever-growing body
Distancing itself from a female body
This body, a hated body, an ignored body,

Body in rebellion, dying so slowly body

This body, my body, male-born body

This body given a second chance to grow
A new body blooming from the old body
A body bringing its reflection into focus
A body mirroring the body of its mother

This body, my body, Trans-Girl body

Sticks And Stones, They Say

Staring at the distorted

Reflection of myself

Within the shattered glass

Of my wounded soul

Sticks and stones they say

They may break my bones

But words

Words can never hurt you

And here I am

Broken and shattered

In places only I can see

In ways only words can

Sticks and stones they say

They may break my bones

But words

Are able to cripple the soul

Jessica Jaymes Purdy

I Like The Way She Looks[x]

When you are perceived as male

And say, *"I like the way she looks"*

The assumption people make

Is that you are attracted to her beauty

But others, mostly men, be they young or old,

Will say, *"I'd hit that ass too."* And let's be honest

That's probably the least demeaning language

You will hear from men who feel entitled to crudeness

This ownership and objectification of women

This is male privilege being passed along

From one generation to another

Spreading like a sickness from man to man

But, when I would say, *"I like the way she looks"*

I meant "*I wish that I looked like her; was her*"

Maybe if I had felt safer among them

I wouldn't have traded my silence for passing

Silent Secret

57

All these long years

I've held a truth

I've kept it close

      Secret

      Silent

All these long years

I've nurtured

This truth

      Secretly

      Silently

Jessica Jaymes Purdy

Only For Them

The hollow sound of happiness

Scratching against silence

It's a shattered illusion

Just a plastic smile

On display for those

Who never really wanted

To know the truth just below

The mask I wore only for them

Cellular Life And Its Impact On The Soul

From the vastness of eternity

I looked down at the small fragile marble

Of blue and green and brown;

Its white clouds bearing witness

To the lives of the souls beneath them.

And like the clouds, I watched and witnessed

Until the day I recognized the woman

Who would become my mother.

When the cells of my soon-to-be body began,

I felt their pull; their promise of home.

And I whispered hello to my mother's soul.

I spoke with her of possibilities, of lives and love.

I spoke with her of womanhood.

I shared in her worries, her fears, and her dreams.

And for 9 months she dreamed me into being.

Oh, but the universe has a of sense of humor

And lessons for us to learn that it holds close

Until it believes it's time to begin.

And so the woman I had thought to be

Was born into cells that divided into X and Y.

This was so not what I had planned or foreseen.

But this was to be the body, my body. Male body.

My journey, it's lessons suddenly included a master's course

In finding strength within and living authentically.

My life would become my soul's thesis

Cellular Life and Its Impact on the Soul

An exploration of biological imperatives

When in opposition to a soul's authentic being.

And 40 years in, I know my body does not rule the soul.

Derailed

Derailed

Frustrated annoyed

The worry mounts and rides
Anxiety like a blown lathered horse

Rock fall on the tracks
Train too slow to stop

Derailed

Scattered distracted

Questions of self-worth swim
Angry oceans like ravenous sharks

Tidal wave cresting
Shallow hull capsizing

Jessica Jaymes Purdy

Derailed

62

Falling Drowning

In doubt and insecurity

Beneath the weight of worry

Mirrors Lie

There are those who say that mirrors never lie.

But they are only shiny veneer behind a polished lens, offering an
illusion of reality.

There are those who say that a mirror never lies.

But they have never stared into it's thin copy of reality, looking for
the depth of their own soul.

There are those who say that a mirror never lies.

But they have never resided within that image, trapped in
someone else's truth.

There are those who say that a mirror never lies.

But they have only ever seen the beauty that they have wanted to
believe.

There are those who say that mirrors never lie.

But they are only shiny veneer behind a polished lens, offering an
illusion of reality.

Jessica Jaymes Purdy

Behind Tinted Glass

If happiness is bright pinks

And deep purples

Mine was only visible

Through dark tinted windows

It was a happiness that was seen

More easily by those who

Closed the distance between us

But could never be felt

My happiness was always

Locked away behind that

Tinted glass and it's warm touch

Never reached beyond the glass

Hiding Behind Manhood

When you hide

You hide

Behind a frown; a scowl

Lips pressed tight

Hooded eyes

You hide

Behind non-committal

Guttural sounds; shrugging shoulders

Arms still at your side

You hide

In blacks and blues

Colors dull

And forgettable

Jessica Jaymes Purdy

Hello Truth

I am alone within myself.

Alone with the truth of who I am

All these long years

I've kept it secret

A quiet truth

Shared with none

I am alone within myself

But others have been alone as well

After all these long years

They've begun to share

Their secret truths

We are not alone

I am alone within myself

But I'm beginning to see the truth

Shooting Stars & Origami Swans

After all these long years

I'm finding my voice

And my truth

Is growing too large to hold

I am alone within myself

But not alone in the world

After all these long years

It's time to share

My truth

Hello,

I'm Jessica Jaymes

Jessica Jaymes Purdy

Slipping Mask

One day the mask will slip

And you will glimpse beneath

How long will we last then?

Who I am is not a lie

Neither hidden nor revealed

I am the man you know

The woman trapped and hiding

One day you will meet a piece

Of her and the me that hides beneath

How long will we last then?

Who I am is the mask

And the man I display

The woman within

Defines the man without

My Silence

Over the years I've gotten good at silence

I learned to pretend and became a master

I taught myself how to ignore

And still stand upon my moral ground

But failed to see how badly I failed the world

And those who needed from me, more

I told myself that my silence only lent strength

To my voice when I choose to speak

But failed to realize that a gift seldom used

Is never practiced enough to succeed

I was always so good at pretending that hurtful words

Were just a difference of opinion or a lack of understanding

I failed to see just how deep those roots were

And how those words bloomed from callous hearts.

Jessica Jaymes Purdy

Over the years I've gotten good at silence

I learned to pretend and became a master

A master at being a fool

DREAMS OF FREEDOM

Jessica Jaymes Purdy

Gossamer Wings

Close my eyes

Dreaming from the soul

Stained glass gossamer wings

Bloom and flutter

The heavy bones

Of who I am dissolve

Into bright light

And infinite strength

I'm lifting up and away

Over the rainbow

Through the misty veil

To a place I'll be forever free

Just As Eve Freed Herself[+]

I spent too long accusing myself of crimes other people believed in

But my body is not a prison

And I am not a sin

My love is not perverse

It is pure

I will no longer shackle myself to the beliefs of people who speak of love

From hearts that offer only hate

Because their sin

Is 'forgiven' through a perversion

Of repentance

I have freed myself from the bondage of other people's limiting beliefs

Re-created my body in my own

Self-image just as Eve

Freed herself from God's garden

And claimed her sovereignty

Jessica Jaymes Purdy

All I Need To Hear

I grew up being your son

And all through the years

I heard the words I love you

Precede it, and I knew it was true

But inside my heart was a daughter

Longing to hear the words I love you

You would have told her had you known the truth

Now, as I begin to become that lonely girl inside

We hear the words I love you followed by son

And wonder why we feel so confined

One day, I'll be your daughter

And for all our remaining years

I hope to hear the words I love you

Precede, who I've become

Shooting Stars & Origami Swans

For now, though, I'm

Somewhere in between

I'm not yet your daughter

So much more than your son

And all I need to hear is I love you.

Jessica Jaymes Purdy

Braids

Braids are a dream of a day yet to come when my womanhood
has grown longer than a year-old shaggy haircut, and fingers have
become practiced at weaving woman from the masculine.

Braids are the girl growing up who lived only in dreams finally
seeing her reflection only after she's aged into her middle years.

Braids are a promise that the heart may play,
at any age, the games if growing and maturing.

Braids are knots that do not bind and yet hold within their
repetitive pattern the DNA of a dream finally being born.

Braids are everything to someone who's never been permitted
them and just another way of being for those who have always
possessed what I most desired.

Shooting Stars & Origami Swans

Braids are a skill I've yet to master, for I've not yet exited my

awkward puberty of becoming.

Braids are a daughter's hair that has been folded with love by her

Mother's swift hands or daddy's cautious overthinking fingers.

Braids are a dream of a moment that never existed

but won't be denied breath.

Braids are a meditation of self-care and self-creation.

Braids are one day going to be reflected in my mirror along with a

with a smile born of a moment that's waited for near to forever.

Jessica Jaymes Purdy

Exhale

How long I held the breath of living

In lungs that sobbed, choking

On not really living at all,

Drowning in existing through

Days that were dirges sung;

Born of my own dying.

How long I held that final breath

Afraid to exhale and follow

The last of my warmth

Into to the cold, dark night,

Drawing out the keening dirge

That I had become.

How long I held that breath,

Full of sadness and despair,

Dying beautifully,

Forever a shadow of life,

A memory of the song

That once was me.

Shooting Stars & Origami Swans

I held that breath ever so long,

Long enough for my lungs

To quake in exhaustion

And my song to falter;

That I no longer remembered

That exhaling was possible.

I held that last and final breath

Until my heart began to beat

In a rhythm that drowned

The dirge that I had become

In an encomium symphony

To every memory I had of living.

I held the breath of living

Until I forgot that I was dying,

Until I remembered living,

Until I was strong enough

To open my mouth and let go

Of the dirge my life had become.

And when I finally let go of that final breath,

That final exhale, I could breathe again

And I knew that I was not dying, never had been;

That the dirge I had been was one of not living;

That death was not yet part of my song, never had been;

That living was something I could still choose.

Until It Wasn't

It was enough

To know and understand

It was enough

Just to accept myself

It was enough

Until it wasn't

It was enough

Just to hang with the girls

It was enough

To go shopping

And watch them buy

The clothes I could never wear

It was enough

Until it wasn't

Jessica Jaymes Purdy

It was enough

To help raise the boys

It was enough

To be the mother

They called father

It was enough

Until it wasn't

It was enough

To live as myself only at home

It was enough

To toss my pants

Into the hamper

And wear my skirts

Alone at home

It was enough

Until it wasn't

Shooting Stars & Origami Swans

It's not enough

I'm tired of pretending

Tired of being alone

Tired of living one life

And another at home

It was enough

Until it wasn't

It's not enough

What Part Of Me Must Die

How do I do this?

How do I become

The woman I was

Always meant to be

When I've never been

The girl I've always dreamed

Where do I begin?

How do I end?

What part of me

Must die

So that the rest

Of me can live

Morning Fullness

I fill my morning with the unpacking

Of half-remembered dreams;

Worries carried in from yesterday;

Plans for the day that I've not yet built.

I fill my morning with wonderment

At my body's changing shape,

With the love and care we now share

As we journey to becoming whole.

I fill my morning with the words

Of friends and family, and words of strangers;

With words of love and compassion,

Carefully locking the gates around my heart

To protect against the now inescapable words,

Words of hate, of anger, words that wound.

I fill my morning with coffee and fruit;

With morning doses of womanhood

Packed into small, almost minty magic;

With orbiting the gravity of my body.

Jessica Jaymes Purdy

I fill my morning with closets thrown open

And curtains pulled back to reveal the light;

With colors and shapes bought to showcase

The fullness and beauty of who I've become.

Overthrown

Born into a body that meant

I must love blue and all things war;

That football and baseball

Were what I should enjoy

Rather than baking or dancing.

Born into a time I could not be seen

Because my elders were stealth;

Passing unseen, quietly living

Lives after attempts to overthrow

Culture became sanitized.

Born without words of knowing,

I waged war upon myself,

(Like a good little boy)

Trying to overthrow my soul

And occupy her life with manhood.

Jessica Jaymes Purdy

Born as one to be another,

I fought a civil war that raged

Until at 20, a bomb dropped

With a single word of truth. Transgender.

And then, I was no longer losing.

But, as I marched on my sadness,

Intent on overthrowing my pain,

The battle shifted from civil to

World. Society was not ready

For who I would one day become.

And in the end, the civil war turned

As I overthrew my soul,

Made of her a prisoner,

Starved and tortured her,

And lived once more clad in blue.

Shooting Stars & Origami Swans

Twenty years later, in the news

Came word of others whose civil wars

Had brought their true selves into power

And were now campaigning

To free lost souls from cages.

And they sent words of hope

That picked the locks on my soul;

Releasing her to try, once more,

To overthrow learned masculinity

And reclaim the throne of womanhood.

This time, I did not wage war.

I used compassion and forgiveness;

Truly overthrowing, in that act of love,

The pain, and sadness, and fear

That held me captive for so long.

Jessica Jaymes Purdy

Torn Pages

Dark shadowed thoughts

Spreading like spilled ink

Eclipsing the bright white

Page of hope torn hurriedly

Out of the notebook I record

My life in. Memories scribbled

Into forever, sometimes boundless

On the narrow-lined paper of my soul.

Turn the page to start a new chapter.

Flip backward in time, searching

For things I've forgotten or wish that I had.

This torn page like a stutter in the telling -

An ending that wasn't but might have been.

91

How many pages of hope have I torn from myself?

How many more pages have I left crumpled

And discarded, hoping that someone

Might find them, flatten them out with gentle

Loving hands, and read through the scribbles

And sorrowful ink stain despair and see

Beneath it all that I just need to hear someone

Say, *"I see you now. You are no longer alone."*

Jessica Jaymes Purdy

Plunge Of The Needle

I wake once more

On the Saturday after last

Feeling the anticipation

Of changes to come

Of a future crafted

In my own self-image

It's time once more

To plunge the needle

Of my becoming deep

Into my own thigh

And inject another dose

Of me into myself

To Look In The Mirror And Not Be Dreaming[x]

The past is full of tangled memories

Of bodies I dreamed to inhabit

And the one to which I was born.

Of course I liked looking

At the magazine hidden

At the bottom of my drawer.

So much I wanted what I saw.

Not to possess or to use.

But this is where it gets tangled,

Because everyone assumed

That I must look upon them

With lust in my loins

And a desire to strip them down;

To press their flesh into mine

In sweaty, primal ecstasy;

To own them as a man owns

A woman the moment

He shackles her with a ring.

But this is where it gets tangled.

Because I so much wanted

What I saw, to possess and to use.

Because I dreamed, one day,

That I might become them,

With their beauty and easy grace.

Because I didn't want to

Have their flesh pressed

Against mine so much as

I wanted their flesh as my own;

To stand in front of a mirror and not

Be dreaming of a magazine model.

Waiting To Change

95

We all change with time

Our faces crease and fold

Beneath the weight of our worries

And wisdom chases gray through our hair

As our hearts forever chisel our hardened edges into a soft, supple caring

But some of us change more;

Change without changing;

Awakening from within, a vision

Of ourselves for the world to finally see;

A vision we've seen in dreams but never mirrors

And held in silence, waiting

Waiting for you to change with time

Jessica Jaymes Purdy

Dreaming Myself Into Existence

I'm dreaming myself into existence

From bones I once called home

Though they ever felt as though

They were a jailer's cell

I'm dreaming myself into existence

A beautiful, bright fairy goddess

Who's wings of stained gossamer

Spread invisibly behind me

Lifting me from the shadows of my life

A Warrior Born

Jessica Jaymes Purdy

I Have Always Been

In the beginning

I fidgeted and fussed

I squirmed and giggled

And cried and wept

I wailed

In the beginning

I was admonished, corrected

I was scolded and disciplined

There were harsh tones and angry words

Whispered rage

Then I learned

To sit still and be silent

I became a ghost, invisible

I hid in plain sight, pretending

All the while

Shooting Stars & Origami Swans

Then I learned

When to move and when to speak

I became every expectation

Every stereotype trope

Of a man

Today, I tell you

I will not sit nor be silent

I will not hide or be ignored

I will not blend or just pretend

For you

Today, I tell you

I am fierce, and I am free

I am angry and determined

I am rising in righteous indignation

I am

And always have been

A woman

Wild Woman

Wild woman, you beat within my breast when I was young;

Fought to be seen when all I wanted was to hide.

You raged at the constraints it placed upon us.

You wept at the names they called us.

You wanted to be heard.

You wanted to be known,

But you were chained in the shadow of masculinity.

You fought until we grew tired.

You lit the eternal flame

That warmed the depths of my soul

While I suffered through my own hellish winter.

You rested in your weariness

Gathering strength, waiting for your time to come again;

To rise once more. Never defeated; strategizing.

You let the world and time shift around you.

You heard the stories of those weeping in shame

For the women that they would be.

You heard the stories of atrocity at the hands of patriarchy

And your righteous anger grew

Until your long silent lips let loose the flames of rage

And you rose once more.

Wild woman, you've beat within my breast for as long as I have lived

Though I named you not to the world.

Now we rise as one, our truth the blade

Beneath which the patriarchy shall fall

As we declare our birthright without shame. Without fear.

We are women. We live.

We will not remain hidden.

Jessica Jaymes Purdy

She Waited

So many moments have passed

Captured in memory

Of a person in a body

That we all thought was mine

But it wasn't, and I knew that

Deep within my soul

Was a person without

A body to call her very own

So many moments have passed

Fading memories

As she waited for

Her time to be born anew

Ascendant Woman

He recedes into the shadows

A dream once reality

Fading into memory

Eclipsed by her bright soul

Shining in defiance

Ascending to her throne

Claiming by right of birth

What he pretended

Was his alone

She is a warrior princess

The patient midwife

A powerful Sorceress

Giving birth to herself

Creating her life from his

Claiming her place

Jessica Jaymes Purdy

Wisdom

My wisdom is scar tissue

Formed in hard, bright lines

Coursing across and through my soul

Like the veins that bled bright red

As I battled through life lessons

While collecting a suit of protective armor

Piece by hard-won piece

Until, fully armored, I realized

The armor was as dangerous

As life itself and less useful

Discarded, it stands in memory

A shiny, battered source of wisdom

I reflect on as I stand naked and scarred

In the center of life -Living- -Loving-

You call me wise; I doubt that wisdom

I've never claimed to be wise

Shooting Stars & Origami Swans

All I know is that I once lived as a child

That the village was not enough to save me

When the brigands came for my innocence and joy

That I survived by learning how to take a blow

To deflect an attack - to conceal and surprise

I learned to lose battles and win wars

I learned that I was alone beneath my armor

I learned that I needed a village

I learned to live without my armor

I learned to live

Finally understanding

That I had been dead

That surviving was not living

That not living was death

I learned that I died in that first village

That I had become an angry, fearful, lonely spirit

Haunting the spaces where I was supposed to be alive

If that is wisdom . . .

Jessica Jaymes Purdy

Stained Glass Warrior

There was a time long ago

Where I fought with brutal anger

Viscous in my attacks

As I sought to destroy

All that made me fearful

Made me different

And forever unwelcome

I was heavy with the armor I wore

Believing I could survive anything

But I had mistaken my rage

For strength and surviving for living

But the harder I fought

And the more I raged

The more of myself I lost

And so I retreated into myself

Making a fortress of my soul

Heavy with stone and mortar

All access to my heart denied

Shooting Stars & Origami Swans

But even there behind my walls

I could not escape the battle

Raging within the confines

Of my self-made prison fortress

Neglecting the life that was mine

As I slowly crumbled in on myself

A broken, defeated soul

Lost and alone in the darkness

My soul spent and empty

I became a shadow

Haunting the life I wasn't living

The warrior I had thought

Myself to be died

Leaving only broken pieces

As I lay despairing

Amongst the rubble of my being

I dreamt of all that I had lost

And all that had never been

And I became an alchemist

Turning stone to glass

I became a priestess

Sanctifying my wounds

With forgiveness and love

Making gold of my suffering

Prayerfully rekindling the fires of hope

I filled all the wounds

In my soul with gold

Replaced the heavy sadness

With stained glass color

I relit the fire of my soul

Allowing the beauty of my suffering

To shine with truth

Rather than fighting them

With the darkness within

I overcame the shadows

With the light of my hope and love

Shooting Stars & Origami Swans

I've become a

Stained Glass Warrior

Fighting with the light

Of hope and love

Knowing my strength

Lies not in being inviolable

But in being unconquerable

I've become a

Stained Glass Warrior

Jessica Jaymes Purdy

Let It All Burn

The beautiful garden of my soul

Trampled and overrun

With the invasive weeds

Of other's hateful, hurtful words

Plowed it under - built a fortress

With high, unassailable walls

Hardened defenses protecting

A princess locked in a tower room

She's discovered her power

Going to let it all burn to the ground

To rise in strength and beauty

From the fiery feathers of flame

Sacred Reliquary

Just because my body is sacred

Doesn't mean I've always loved it

> At times
>
> I've
>
> Hated
>
> It

Because the vessel was a denial of me

Yes

My body is sacred

So is change

Just because my body is sacred

Doesn't mean I can't ask it to

> Change
>
> Become
>
> Reflect
>
> Be

All that my soul truly is and honor me

Jessica Jaymes Purdy

Yes

My body is sacred

So is change

Because my body is sacred

I chose to shape it in the image of me

    The

    Sacred

    Soul

    Within

Bringing forth the beauty of authentic self

Yes

My body is sacred

So was its change

Warrior Princess

I'm a warrior princess.

I've always been a warrior.

For a long time, I was a warrior without a war. So, I waged war on myself and those who tried to love me.

That I didn't have a war is not really true. I had a war. I just didn't know how to fight it. In the end I laid waste to everything. I destroyed relationships. I destroyed my body and my health. I destroyed my careers.

I didn't know which battles to fight, so I fought them all or fought none. I fought like a berserker. No thought. No plan. Just fury and anger unleashed. Or I didn't fight and stood upon the parapet of the fortress I had made of myself looking out from my self-imposed siege.

I'm a warrior princess.

I've always been a warrior.

And I'm only now beginning to learn what being a warrior princess means. I'm only now learning how to be the warrior I've always been.

DEFIANCE

Jessica Jaymes Purdy

To Exist

I existed once

Before they taught me

To be a boy

And repress all that I was

I exist again

And have become a teacher

A woman

Teaching authenticity

By existing

Without apology

Prayer For Today

I pray that people see only me

And not the turmoil roiling

My oceanic soul.

I pray that my depths absorb

The storm and calm the churning

Seas of my mind.

I pray that people understand

The secrets I hold keep safe the sails

Of my strength

I pray that my skies will soon clear

Of the doubts and fears clouding

The horizon of my dreams

Shhhhh now, while I pray and plan

I'm charting my course

Out of the storm

Jessica Jaymes Purdy

I Am More[x]

I'm more than what you see;

So much more.

I'm more

Than a box checked M;

The dangling piece of meat

You imagine within my pants

When you hear my name

Or see my face.

I'm so much more than what you see.

I'm a goddess

In the shadows;

A princess in waiting.

I'm a mother waiting for birth.

So much more than what you see.

So. Much. More.

Shooting Stars & Origami Swans

I'm a thousand

Dreams being dreamt;

A million moments still to come.

I'm a memory

For all whom I've ever met;

A promise yet to come.

I'm so much more than what you see.

I'm a man on the outside

And a girl

Living - dreaming - breathing

Inside myself

Waiting like a caterpillar

To become a beautiful butterfly.

I'm so much more;

More than you have ever seen.

Jessica Jaymes Purdy

Tomorrows***

I can't remember now

The first time I didn't want to see

Tomorrow

There were so many

So many tomorrows

Drowning in tears

I can't remember exactly when

Tomorrow came and I no longer

Felt crushed beneath its weight

There's been so many since

So many tomorrows

I've lived with pride

It Is I Who Decides

Who's to say who I am?

Other than me?

Who's to say that I cannot exist

As I am, which is

Not some trivial claim

Nor a delusion

A fabrication

Or a lie

Who's to say who I am?

Other than me?

It's not you who decides if I can exist

As the person I am

It is I who decides, unreservedly,

To honor myself

Acknowledge myself

My womanhood.

Jessica Jaymes Purdy

Truth & Boundaries ≠ Militant

I asked you to use my chosen name

I insisted you use the pronouns

That reflect my gender identity

And I repeat myself

      And I repeat myself

           And I repeat myself

I go about my day being visible

I go out of my way to politely

Respond to questions asked

And I repeat myself

      And I repeat myself

           And I repeat myself

I am upfront about who I really am

I am asking only for respect

And the right for me to exist

Shooting Stars & Origami Swans

And I repeat myself

    And I repeat myself

        And I repeat myself

I point out the discrimination I regularly face

I point out how you could do more

And I keep calm until you push

And I repeat myself

    And I repeat myself

        And I repeat myself

I point out the harm that actions have

I point out how to avoid causing more

And I repeat myself over again

And I repeat myself

    And I repeat myself

        And I repeat myself

You call me militant for demanding respect

You call me militant for calling out harm

And making you feel uncomfortable

Because you are not listening

Because you are complicit

Because you are toxic

My Womanhood

My womanhood is a million tears

That bled from veins weeping in secret

While dry eyes became stony with anger

Mistaken for absolute proof of masculinity

My aggression was dismissed as "boys will be boys"

Until I became a dangerous weapon

Turned, no longer inward, but into a war

Raging beyond the borders of my own flesh

Turning love to ash in scorched earth rages

My womanhood is a word discovered

Before the world was ready to understand

Held in secret, chained in solitary confinement

Because worshipping at the altar of authenticity

Was an outlawed paganism and mortal sin

In a world where we were all supposed to be one

And our differences became guarded borders

Bristling with aggressive bigotries

That kept me as a prisoner of war within myself.

My womanhood is a fierce compassion

That I baptized everyone but myself in

Making my love a prayer of worship

Sanctifying the wounded hearts

Of those whose pain were echoes of my own

The prayer of healing and forgiveness I became

Mirrored the prayers I never sent for myself

Choosing instead to suffer penance for sins

I never committed, but I was assured were mine

My womanhood was the breath of life

Singing songs of love I could not understand

Within this body I called home but never mine

Shooting Stars & Origami Swans

Until the day when the stories of other women

Sharing my journey rang like a clarion call

Beckoning me to accept my place within our community

To worship our true selves despite the fear

Of persecution as heretics who blasphemed

The orthodoxy of womanhood the patriarchy believed

Jessica Jaymes Purdy

A Beautiful Fucking Weed[+]

She told me that there was a place in God's garden for everyone.

But only if I grew within the bounds of who she believed I should be;

only if I agreed to be pruned like a delicate little flower,

confined to the narrow rules of the beliefs she held.

He told me that I was a snowflake because I stood up to him,

his privilege, his prejudice, and his bigotry;

because I did not fit within his narrow view

of who was worthy of God's love.

But the only resemblance I have to the snowflake

is that I am a beautiful individual

unique from anyone else in the gardens of God.

They told me that there was no lasting place for me in God's garden;

that I did not belong, that there could only be a place for me if I agreed

to be tamed and pruned,

and made to fit a very narrow view of personhood;

that there was only a place in God's garden for me

if I agreed to not be me at all.

And because I will not, they swear I will go to hell.

But I am not a snowflake or a delicate little flower.

There is not a place for me in these carefully curated gardens of God,

for I am a beautiful fucking weed.

Strong. Resilient. Wild. Untamed.

I can survive the wilderness, and in uncertainty.

I can survive in the chaos of the wild of the places

where the delicate flowers worry about being trampled.

I can survive without their God's garden gloves and watering can.

I can do more than survive; I can thrive.

And that is why they fear me.

They fear my resilience, my ability to survive in the spaces they fear.

They fear that if they let me in, I will destroy

the tamed sameness of their walled garden of God,

for they know that if I ever do enter their garden,

I will not be confined to my place in their narrow view of the world

or allow myself to be pruned and shaped

and made into something other than me.

No, if I ever agree to take root in their garden,

I will be the beautiful fucking weed that makes the roses weep.

Misogynistic Wasteland, Part 1: Blizzard Rising

You took me for granted

As if I were clear blue skies,

You who sailed the barren, dry sands

Of the misogynistic wasteland

Our society has seemingly always been.

So often, I was like a heat mirage.

You mistook me for just another guy

An oblivious, privileged patriarch.

Oh, the things I've heard you say

When you thought you were safe.

And when I turned to cloudy gray skies

Confusion danced across your face

As you struggled to comprehend

The betrayal of being called out

And the changing of my face.

I questioned your authority,

Refused to be confined

To the masculine role assigned.

I demanded better treatment

For myself and women in general.

Unwilling to change or grow;

Unable to accept that society

Is sailing beyond the barren, dry sands

Of your misogynistic wasteland,

You watched in fear, my cloudy gray skies.

I, who you once dreamed

Was a snowflake destined to melt,

Became a fierce storm raging,

Rocking your journey through

Privileged comfort and ease.

Shooting Stars & Origami Swans

But I was not a single angry cloud

Storming with rage alone.

On every horizon, we were gathering,

And now I could see your confusion

Giving way to realization and panic.

Trapped, now, in the blizzard

Of those who've had enough,

Who will no longer be silent,

Who demand to be treated with respect,

You've begun to see my true face.

Our saga is far from over.

Jessica Jaymes Purdy

Once Again: I'm A Beautiful Fucking Weed

I've said it once

      I'll say it again

I'm a beautiful fucking weed

I'll push against the base of the concrete until it cracks wide open

I'll force my way through in defiance and blossom

I'll resist every effort at eradication

I can last the drought and thrive in the first drop of rain

I can be mowed down and spring back in just moments

A time-lapse ode to growth and resilience

I've said it once

      I'll say it again

I'm a beautiful fucking weed

      I will persist

A JOYFUL WOMAN

Jessica Jaymes Purdy

Another Day Of Hope

Insidious

The doubt lurks

    Just out of sight   In the shadows.

    It creeps   Slowly   Silently

Suddenly pouncing

Like you are prey   The weakest of the herd

    But you were alone when it struck

    Separated from the protective

    Love and care

    Of those who call you theirs

But would it have made a difference?

    Would not the doubt have struck even then?

    Would not the doubt have singled you out?

Shooting Stars & Origami Swans

Struck you down   Grasped you by the neck
                           With its powerful jaws
Maybe   Maybe someone might have noticed
           And helped you fight back the doubt

But

You were alone when it struck   Paralyzed

Weak and afraid   Defeated.   But not
    Somewhere   Deep within   Hope kindled
    Strength

You were alone when you fought back
Alone when you remembered

Your strength   Your worthiness

You were alone   When
You remembered   You

And won another day

Of hope

Except

I'd do it differently

Except for that time

I kissed my first girlfriend

In the hall between class

Tasting the cinnamon on her tongue

Only to lose her later to someone "more"

I'd do it differently

Except for that time

I joined the Army and left

Home not knowing exactly

Who I was or what truths I'd be hiding

Only to find myself discharged under Don't Ask, Don't Tell

I'd do it differently

Except for that time

I was standing on my porch

Having life-altering visions

Wondering how I had survived

While so many friends overdosed

Jessica Jaymes Purdy

I'd do it differently

Except for that time

I said the words, "I do"

To the woman who would leave

My carefully constructed self-image

Shattered for a man who was "more"

I'd do it differently

Except for that time

I became a stay-at-home

Parent to children not my own

When my best friend was deploying

To Afghanistan, and I could not work

I'd do it differently

Except for that time

I said this is who I am

Risking friendships and

Career alike to finally live fully

And unapologetically as myself

I'd do it differently

Except. . .

Jessica Jaymes Purdy

Sisters of Shared Experience

I never had a sister growing up.

Though I begged for one,

Always knowing

A part of me needed sisterhood.

But today. Today, I am a sister.

And I hope I'm the kind

Of sister

That I always prayed to find.

I'm surrounded by sisters

Of shared experience,

There for them

Just as they are there for me.

Sometimes we're sisters;

Outside looking in.

A lonely

Collective sisterhood.

Shooting Stars & Origami Swans

Sometimes we're sisters

Warmly welcomed

By women

Born into a lifetime of sisterhood.

But always, we are sisters in spirit,

Sharing strength and

Experience,

Lifting each other up in sisterhood.

Jessica Jaymes Purdy

Both

I am a body and a soul

I am both feminine

And not

>How I both hate

>And love that

I tried to be one

While desperate

To become the other

The journey from one to the other

Is a lesson in loving both

>The experience of before

>The promise of the future

I am a body and a soul

The journey from one to the other

Will not erase all that I was before

How I both hate

And love that

I love who I've become

The changes of body

The loss of sorrow

I am both beginning

And continuing

Becoming myself

Without losing who I was

I am a body and a soul

Jessica Jaymes Purdy

Enchanted Princess Wakes

The enchanted princess wakes

Bleary-eyed and dazed

Wondering why the curse now lifted

Was cast at all and by whom

She wakes from dream to dream

Nightmares that tossed her on masculine shores

Nightmares that will test her soul in a storm

She wakes from dream to dream

This enchanted princess blessed

With a second point of view

Wondering why no one else could see

The curse that was and is no more

Blessed she walks from life to life

A life of hiding and denying her feminine soul

A life beginning from masculine bone

Blessed she walks from life to life

Shooting Stars & Origami Swans

An enchanted princess living

A fairytale story told in whispered tones

Her story of strife of courage of love

And a curse that strengthened her soul

Jessica Jaymes Purdy

My New Colors

Like autumn trees

I'm changing

New colors redefine

Who the world sees

The dying leaves

Of who I was falling away

Like spring flowers

I'm blossoming

New colors redefine

Who the world sees

The delicate petals

Of my soul finally on display

My Life Isn't Short

Life is short, and starting it over would seem to make it all the shorter.

But no. Not really.

Not in the ways that really count.

No, my life isn't shorter for having missed so much of it.

For having lost so much of it to not getting it right.

No, starting over gave me a new lease on life.

A continuation of the one I hadn't been living.

It gave me new joy. New love. New worth. New time.

Time, I had thought to give away. To leave unused.

Time I was sure I didn't want. That would be too painful. To purposeless.

And as short as my new lease on life may be,

It's not short at all. Not really.

Not in the ways that count.

Not short on joy. Not short on laughter. Not short on love.

No, it's not short at all now that I've started over and really begun to live.

Life is short, they say.

Never wait to do or say what your heart demands.

And maybe that's true.

But my life isn't short at all.

A Holy Testament

My bruised body

Is a thing of beauty

The purple blossoming

From the incision

Where the surgeon

Removed the masculine flood

That swept over me like a tsunami

And left me drowning

The pain of this body

Is a holy testament

To the Divine gift

Of self-determination

And the sacredness

Of honoring your soul

Of loving yourself

Of living your truth

The Storm And The Oasis

When I was a small child

I was ocean waves crashing

On sandy beaches where

Friends and family would

Come and play in my joy

Or surf my happy exuberance,

Even though sometimes

My riptides pulled them under

And carried them far from

My happy shores.

But I will be at peace.

It's seemed that every year

My waves would grow,

Crashing a little harder,

Carrying away more and more

Of my happy beaches

Until one day my waves

Reached into the sky

Shooting Stars & Origami Swans

And became a turbulent storm

Full of angry lightning

And raging thunder

The fury of my winds

Cutting destructive paths

Through friendships and family.

But I will be at peace.

Mom became a metrologist

Calculating the strength

And paths of my storms

Issuing warnings for evacuation

Or sheltering in place.

She became a high-pressure system

Pushing my storms out to sea

And offering the storm-weary

A sunny reprieve.

But I will be at peace.

Lost at sea, raging at

The vast, endless, nothing

Of the ocean's depth

I poured myself out.

Monsoon tears falling

From lonely distant horizons.

The salt of my wounded soul

Building new shores

For the sun to shine upon

And the Moon's silver light

To bless and cool.

And I will be at peace.

As I slowly gave birth to myself

I developed lush jungles

Of self-love and found

My shores contained

An abundance of joy

And deep reflecting pools

Shooting Stars & Origami Swans

Of calm tranquility.

And once more, friends and family

Come to play along my happy shores,

For I am no longer crashing waves

With dangerous hidden currents

Or a thundering raging storm.

I have become an oasis.

And finally, I am at peace.

Birthed By Dream

The deepest part of my soul dreamed.

It birthed life and desire, created reality,

A mirror of the truths rising from my depths.

It dreamed that I was Woman, that I could be seen.

It birthed the first steps I would take on my journey;

Nurtured my growing joy and confidence.

The deepest part of my soul dreamed.

It birthed life and desire, created reality,

Granting me freedom and wholeness.

Gender Literacy *

At 3, I didn't understand the differences

Between men and women.

I knew, simply, that I saw myself

Only in my mother and not in my father.

At 5, you could see the differences

Between boys and girls

Only by the clothes they wore

And the colors they chose.

Were they taught to choose

Those colors by parents

Literate only in gender norms

Passed down father to daughter?

I loved purple. I always said blue.

At 9, the playground was divided,

With the boys and girls breaking

Themselves into separate games,

And I stood out among the girls.

Jessica Jaymes Purdy

At 13, I couldn't deny the reasons

Everyone believed I was a boy

As my body was traitorously beginning

The slow process of mirroring my father.

During puberty, I would try to hide from myself

The evidence of a masculinity I didn't desire.

And still, I had no words to define myself;

A boy who wanted desperately to be a girl.

Confusion and silence reign where language fails.

By 14, only hateful words defined me:

Sissy, fag, queer, gay, freak, pussy.

And I became literate in shame,

Self-loathing, despair, and alone-ness.

At 19, a friend introduced me to myself

When they brought the word Transgender

To me as a gift they didn't fully realize

Was the key to the prison of my being.

Shooting Stars & Origami Swans

But at 21, I learned that the world was not ready

For me to become the woman I was born to be

And I became literate in prejudice and denial,

Literate in the safety the closet offered.

I dressed myself in the expected maleness.

Until at 30, my womanhood rose once more,

Urging me to explore the pathways to becoming

The woman that I had for so long denied a life.

But I was not yet literate enough in trust.

By 40, the hateful words of my youth

Had been replaced with new terms

Of hate and fear, replaced with words like

Perversion, predator, man-in-a-dress.

At 41, I became literate in coming out,

In speaking my truth and being myself,

In the differences between sex and gender,

In teaching Gender Literacy to friends and family.

Every conversation became another lesson for me to teach.

42, and I am literate in so many things now:

Joy, wholeness, pride, community, smiling.

I have become literate in loving who I am

And in my own renewed dreams for the future.

Assigned sex, gender identity, gender expression,

Cisgender, gender non-conforming, and asexual,

These words are the language of our new acceptance,

Of our new understanding of gender and sex.

My trans siblings and I, we dream of a bright future;

A future where society has learned to be literate

In tolerance and acceptance, in compassion and inclusion;

A future we hope that you will help us create.

Reflection

The reflection in the mirror

Is changing from day to day

No longer does it reflect my past

Though my family's heritage still shines

The downturned frown shared by generations

Has slowly bent itself upward, reaching for happiness

Jessica Jaymes Purdy

Loving My Womanhood

I love my womanhood

The depths it brings to my emotions

Even when they are drowning me

Even when I don't understand the whys of them

The way that it is shaping my body into a blessing

Now that puberty has come a second time

And my body, my skin, my hair are all softening

The way it dances through me like fire

In response to gentle, loving caresses

How it lingers after in sweet, soft ecstasy

The way it exists beyond definition

A powerful truth living within me

Defying expectations and explanation

This Is Really Me

I'm having one of those *"this is really me days"*

When every time I pass a mirror

Catch my reflection in glass

I'm left staring in wonder

That this is really me

That I have arrived

Finally

At this moment in

My journey to becoming

Who it is that I've always been

That this reflection of a beautiful

Woman is a reflection of my own body

I wonder why I waited so long to be really me

Jessica Jaymes Purdy

Shadows Born of Light

Uncertainty, anxiety

Riding waves from the horizon

Of tomorrow's promise

Dysphoria, loss

Like gray clouds covering the skies

Of tomorrow's promise

Shadows born of light

Leaps of faith, dares accepted

Like golden milk coffee and agave ginger wine

Happy comforts fulfilled

Laughter, friendships

Like silk sheets and velvet blankets

Happy comforts fulfilled

Light eclipses shadow

Living With The Curtains Open

Living with the curtains open

It's an act of courage

An act of self-love

I say this knowing you won't

Understand the truth

Of this simple act

I say this knowing that you

Have always lived with

Open curtains

But the truth is still there

For my home is my

Safe escape

From judging eyes of strangers

Seeing only the body

Of my birth

Jessica Jaymes Purdy

That I'm trying so hard to leave

Behind as I ask it, kindly

To become me

So when I tell you that opening

The curtains of my home

Is courageous

What I'm really saying is this

Home, this safe escape

Became a cell

And the courageousness

Of throwing open

The curtains

And daring to be visible within

This most sacred, safe

Place I call home

Is indeed an act of self-love

Kintsukuroi Soul

Stained glass soul

Not broken

Shattered

A puzzle pulled apart

Into a thousand tiny pieces

Glowing with light

Too bright to extinguish

With dark intent and painful hurts

Stained glass soul

Not broken

Learning

To puzzle the pieces

Back together into strengthened beauty

Jessica Jaymes Purdy

Glowing with light

Beautiful with gold in all the cracks

My scars become love